Mars

Elaine Landau

Watts LIBRARY

Franklin Watts
A Division of Grolier Publishing
New York • London • Hong Kong • Sydney
Danbury, Connecticut

For Michael, the brightest star in our Universe

Note to readers: Definitions for words in **bold** can be found in the Glossary at the back of this book.

Photographs ©: AKG London: 4 (Engraving by Johann Sadeler); e.t. archive: 20; Finley Holiday Film: 3 bottom, 10, 16, 17, 30, 32, 43; Lowell Observatory Photograph: 22, 23; Lunar and Planetary Institute: 14, 15; NASA: 18 (US Geological Survey, Flagstaff, Arizona), 46 (Image produced by John Frassanito), 38, 41 (JPL), 31 (LPI), 25, 36, 37, 48, 51; Photo Researchers: cover, 6, 7 (US Geological Survey/SPL), 3 top, 12, 27, 39 (NASA/SPL), 19 (SPL), 44 (Detlev Van Ravenswaay/SPL); Photofest: 24; Photri: 28, 33, 34.

Solar system diagram created by Greg Harris

Visit Franklin Watts on the Internet at:
http://publishing.grolier.com

Library of Congress Cataloging-in-Publication Data

Landau, Elaine.
   Mars / Elaine Landau.
      p.   cm.— (Watts Library)
   Includes bibliographical references and index.
   Summary: Reviews the history of Earth's observation of the red planet since ancient times, explores the results of modern scientific studies carried out by telescope, satellite, and landing probe, and speculates on a future human landing.
   ISBN: 0-531-20388-3 (lib. bdg.)   0-531-16428-4 (pbk.)
   1. Mars (Planet)—Juvenile literature. [1. Mars (Planet)] I. Title. II. Series.
QB641.L36 1999
523.43—dc21
                                  98-46327
                                    CIP
                                    AC

Contents

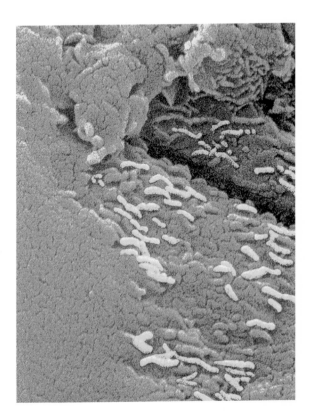

MARS

Mars was named for the ancient Roman god of war.

Chapter One

The Red Planet

The planet Mars appears as a tiny, sparkling, rusty-red ball in the night sky. Humans have been fascinated by this planet for centuries. Some people compare its color to the blood shed in battle. That may be why the ancient Romans named the planet after their god of war. The ancient symbol for the planet Mars —a circle with an arrow—represents the god's shield and spear.

During the Middle Ages, Mars's movements were used to predict the

This color-enhanced view of Mars is made up of more than 100 images taken by the Viking orbiters. Using a computer, the images were fit together like the pieces of a jigsaw puzzle.

outcome of individual battles and entire wars. **Astrologers** looked at Mars's position in the sky before advising rulers about the best time to attack enemies.

Mars is one of the nine planets that make up the **solar system**. The solar system consists of the Sun and the nine planets, dozens of moons, **comets** and **asteroids** that **orbit**, or move around, the Sun. As you can see in the illustration on pages 8 and 9, Mars is the fourth planet from the Sun. Its closest neighbor is Earth.

Mars's Movements

Like all planets in the solar system, Mars orbits the Sun. It takes Mars 687 Earth-days to complete its journey. Earth orbits the Sun in 365 days. Because a year is defined as the amount of time it takes for a planet to revolve around the Sun once, a year on Mars is 687 days long, while a year on Earth is 365 days. Why do you think a Martian year is longer than an Earth year?

Like Earth, Mars experiences seasons and weather changes. Because a Martian year is longer than an Earth year, each Martian season is longer too.

All the objects in our solar system revolve around the Sun because they are trapped by a powerful, but invisible force called **gravity**. The Sun's gravity pulls all the planets and other objects in the solar system toward the Sun. In the same way, Earth's gravity pulls the Moon and everything on our planet toward the center of Earth.

Dozens of images were combined to create this color-enhanced view of Mars. The large white area is a polar ice cap.

The force of gravity operates all around us. For example, when you sit down in a chair, you're able to remain there. Your body does not go floating off into the air. Gravity is what keeps you down. If you toss a coin into a wishing well, it will fall into the water because gravity pulls the coin down. Gravity also causes rain to fall to the ground.

Earth isn't the only planet with gravity. Mars has its own gravitational pull. Because Mars is smaller than Earth, Earth's gravity is stronger than Mars's. The gravitational pull on Earth

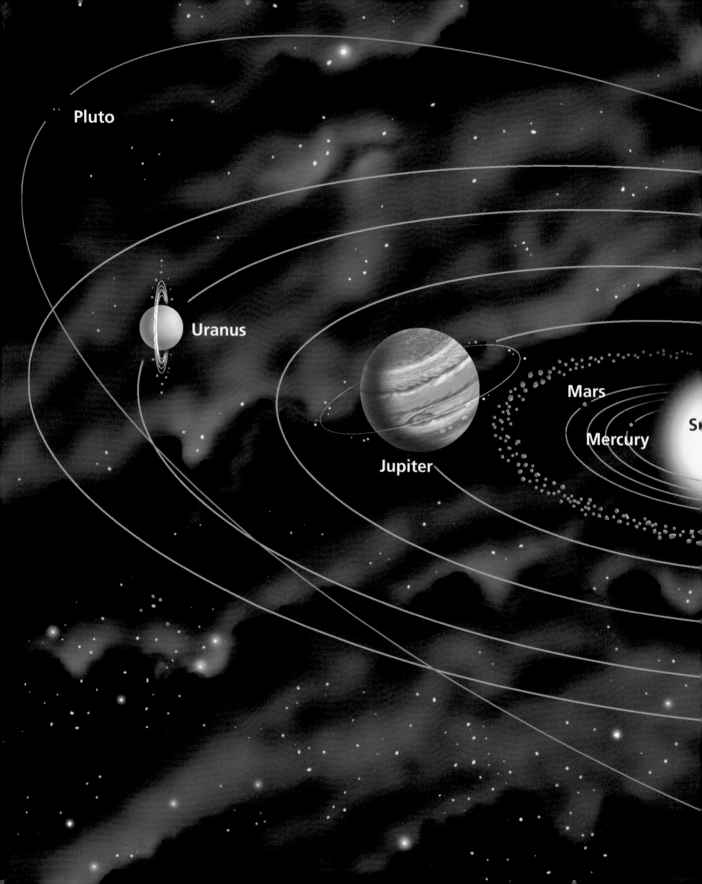

The Solar System

Venus

Moon

Earth

Asteroid Belt

Saturn

Neptune

Although Mars appears quite large in this color-enhanced view, it is actually smaller than Earth.

is about three times greater than it is on Mars. The area over which a planet's gravity extends is called its **gravitational field**.

As Mars orbits the Sun, it also **rotates**, or spins, around its **axis**—an imaginary line through the center of the planet. All planets rotate on an axis like a toy top. Mars rotates once every 24 hours and 37 minutes. Earth rotates once every 23 hours and 56 minutes. That means a day on Mars is just a little longer than a day on Earth.

How Mars Measures Up

Mars is not a very large planet. It's about 4,200 miles (6,790 kilometers) across. Earth is almost twice as large. Since Mars is smaller than Earth, it is made up of less material and has less **mass**. Earth's mass is about ten times greater than that of Mars.

Mars is also less **dense** than Earth. The density of a planet describes the relationship between its mass—the total amount of material in an object—and its **volume**—the total amount of space the object occupies. Earth is the densest planet in the solar system because it has a fairly large mass for its size. Mercury and Venus are also denser than Mars.

The Small Planets

The only planets smaller than Mars are Mercury and Pluto. Mercury is 3,031 miles (4,878 km) across, while tiny Pluto is just 1,430 miles (2,300 km) across.

11

This color-enhanced view of Mars's surface looks similar to a desert on Earth.

Chapter Two

Mars and its Moons

A large portion of Mars's surface is covered by dry, rocky regions that are similar to Earth's deserts, but none of the plants and animals that thrive on Earth could survive on Mars. Because Mars is farther from the Sun, it is much colder than Earth. The average recorded temperature on Mars is –63 degrees Fahrenheit (–58 degrees Celsius). The temperature at Mars's south pole can sometimes fall below –250°F (–157°C).

Temperature isn't the only reason plants and animals can't live on Mars. Even if the red planet were warmer, Earth's creatures couldn't survive because there is no liquid water on the surface of Mars—no oceans, no lakes, and no rivers.

Scientists think there may have been large amounts of water on Mars million of years ago, but now the water supply is either frozen beneath the planet's surface or trapped in the soil and polar ice caps.

These twisting channels on the surface of Mars may have been made by water.

Mars's **atmosphere** is thinner than Earth's and consists mostly of carbon dioxide. The Martian atmosphere also contains small amounts of nitrogen, argon, carbon monoxide, and a few other gases. It has only traces of water vapor and oxygen. Because humans and nearly all other living things need oxygen to live, most of the creatures on Earth could not survive on Mars.

A Closer Look at Mars

If you look at Mars through a telescope, you'll see three different types of **terrain**: bright reddish areas; dark greenish-gray, irregularly shaped areas; and polar ice caps.

The reddish areas cover about two-thirds of the planet's surface. The atmosphere in these areas is dry and dusty, and the land is covered with sand and rocks. These regions are similar to deserts on Earth.

Mars's dark areas, called **marias**, cover about one-third of the planet. *Maria* is the Latin word for "sea," but there is no liquid water in these areas. The size, color, and shape of the marias change throughout the year. Some regions of the marias lighten or even disappear during

This hazy view of Mars through a telescope on Earth shows the red planet's three different terrains.

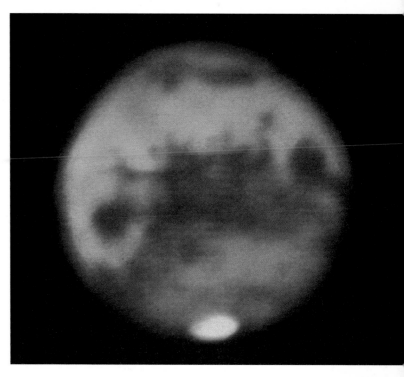

15

the planet's fall and winter seasons, and then darken or reappear during the planet's spring and summer.

Scientists are not sure why marias look different at different times of the year. Some researchers have suggested that the changes may be related to the planet's weather patterns. On Mars, windstorms can last for several weeks. During these storms, winds may blow up to 100 miles (160 km) per hour. The sand and dust picked up and dropped by these strong winds may cover or uncover the dark areas.

Small areas at the north and south poles of Mars are covered by ice caps. From Earth, the ice caps look white. The ice cap at Mars's south pole consists mostly of frozen carbon dioxide. Dust in the ice gives it a slightly reddish tint. Scientists think that most of the northern ice cap is made of frozen water.

Like the marias, the polar caps change in size and shape throughout the year. During the planet's summer, the ice caps shrink. In winter, the ice caps grow larger.

The size of Mars's polar caps varies with the seasons.

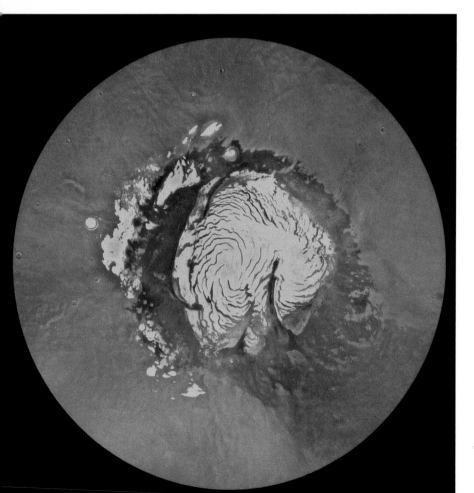

Fantastic Features

To get an even closer look at Mars, you would need to look at photographs taken through a very powerful telescope or by a spacecraft that visited the planet. Such images of the red planet show us that the southern portion of Mars is heavily dotted with **craters**. These large holes were probably formed when huge rocks crashed into the planet millions and millions of years ago. A few of Mars's craters are extremely large. Hellas Basin, one of the largest craters, is so big that the entire state of Texas could easily fit inside it!

We know many of the craters on Mars are very old because they show signs of **erosion**. Over time, the edges and inner surface of these giant holes have been worn away by the planet's strong winds.

Near the planet's **equator** are huge volcanoes. Some are larger than any found on Earth. In fact, Mars's tallest volcano, Olympus Mons, is the largest known volcano in the solar system. It is about three times higher than Mount Everest, the

Dusty Upheavals

Occasionally, great dust storms nearly cover the entire planet. They create large dunes, wind streaks, and wind-carved features on Mars.

This close-up view of Olympus Mons was taken by a Viking orbiter.

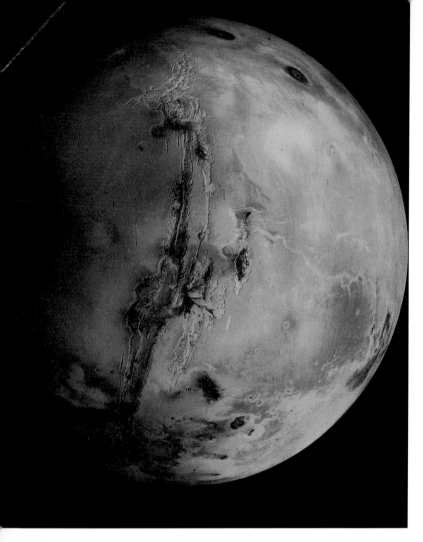

Valles Marineris is more than 1,200 miles (2,000 km) long and up to 5 miles deep (8 km).

tallest mountain on Earth. If Olympus Mons were plopped down in the middle of the United States, its base would stretch all the way from Chicago, Illinois, to St. Louis, Missouri. That's big! This volcano's tremendous size seems even more impressive when you remember that it's located on a planet that is only about half the size of Earth.

Mars also has a huge canyon on its surface. It is called Valles Marineris. In some places, Valles Marineris is 124 miles (200 km) wide, and it is four times deeper than the Grand Canyon in Arizona. Believe it or not, Valles Marineris stretches one-third of the way around the surface of Mars.

Scientists aren't sure how the canyon formed. They think that the land may have split apart as materials deep within the planet shifted. These movements may be similar to the earthquakes we experience on Earth.

Mars's surface also contains features that look like dried-up riverbeds, gorges, and shorelines. These features support the idea that water once flowed on the surface of Mars.

The Moons of Mars

Even though Mars is smaller than Earth, and has a smaller gravitational field, it is orbited by two small, potato-shaped moons. The larger moon is named *Phobos*, which means "fear." At its widest point, Phobos is about 14 miles (22 km) across. It completes one orbit around Mars every 7 1/2 hours. Phobos is slowly moving closer to Mars. Scientists predict that in about 100 million years, Phobos will crash into the red planet. This tiny moon is covered with a layer of dust that is at least 3 feet (1 m) deep. The dust has built up over millions of years as meteorites crash into it.

Mars's other moon is named *Deimos*, which means "panic." At its widest point, Deimos measures about 7 miles (11 km) across. It completes one orbit around Mars every 30 hours.

This color-enhanced view of Phobos orbiting Mars was created by a computer that combined dozens of Viking Orbiter images.

This drawing of Italian astronomer Giovanni V. Schiaparelli shows what he looked like in 1900.

Chapter Three

Is There Life on Mars?

Mars has long been a source of mystery and wonder. For centuries, people have wanted to know whether life existed on the red planet. At one point, some astronomers were convinced that there was intelligent life on Mars.

It all started in 1877—the year Asaph Hall discovered that Mars has two moons. During that year, Mars and Earth were at their closest points to each other while orbiting the Sun. Giovanni V. Schiaparelli, an Italian astronomer, took this opportunity to study Mars's surface in detail. He drew charts and maps of his findings.

Among the features Schiaparelli noted were a great many lines that streaked across the planet's surface. He called these marks **canali**, the Italian word for "channels." In 1878, Schiaparelli published a scientific paper about the Martian channels. As the years passed, he continued to study the channels. He made sketches of the channels and published a number of detailed maps indicating their locations. In all, he identified 113 channels.

Many people were very interested in Giovanni Schiaparelli's work. They wondered if these channels might actually be canals—waterways built by Martians to irrigate crops or transport water to cities. Had the channels been created by intelligent beings?

By 1886, a number of other scientists in the United States, Great Britain, and France had also observed the channels, or canals. One American scientist claimed that he had seen dark spots at the end of some canals. He referred to those areas as "lakes."

An American astronomer named Percival Lowell became obsessed with the idea that these channels were actually canals built by intelligent Martians. To study the channels more closely, Lowell built an observatory—now called Lowell Observatory—in Flagstaff, Arizona. Using the best equipment available, Lowell claimed that he was able to identify at least 500 canals on Mars.

Percival Lowell, an American astronomer, devoted a great deal of time and money to proving that intelligent life existed on Mars.

Lowell designed and built the Lowell Observatory in Flagstaff, Arizona.

Lowell wrote three books describing his ideas about life on Mars. He believed that the Martians were building so many canals because their civilization was threatened by a serious shortage of water on the planet. Lowell thought that the Martians probably built the canals to bring water from Mars's polar ice caps to its drier areas.

In this drawing, Percival Lowell plotted out the canal system he believed Martians built.

Although some astronomers claimed that the canals on Mars were real, others were not convinced. These critics were unable to find the canals. They also noticed that drawings of canal systems made by different astronomers had nothing in common. There were tremendous differences in the widths, lengths, and patterns of the canals.

As a result, a number of scientists argued that the "canals" were probably

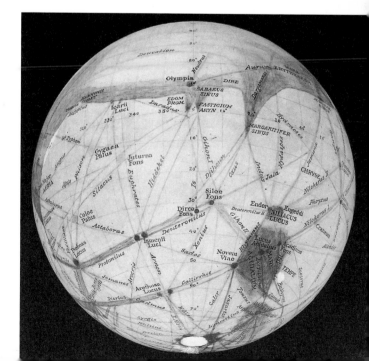

That's Entertainment

Twentieth-century science fiction stories and movies about Martians—little green men—can be traced back to Lowell's ideas. In the early 1900s, books about Martian spaceships landing on Earth could be found in bookstores and libraries across the United States.

In 1938, actor Orson Welles presented a radio play about Martians landing in a small New Jersey town. The broadcast was so convincing that many people panicked. They thought they were hearing an actual news report. Some jumped into their cars and tried to flee. Others locked themselves in their homes. They were terrified by the thought of actually facing invaders from outer space.

nothing more than shadows on the planet's surface. Some suggested that the so-called canals might actually be ridges or sand dunes.

The disagreement about life on the red planet continued for many years. It was not until the first **space probes** visited the planet in the late 1960s and early 1970s that it became clear that there is no intelligent life on Mars. Nevertheless, many scientists continue to believe that some form of life may have existed on Mars millions, or perhaps billions, of years ago.

Microbes in a Martian Meteorite?

In 1984, a team of scientists working in Antarctica came across a 4.2-pound (1.9-kilogram) **meteorite**. They brought it back to the lab and named it ALH84001. When the meteorite was tested, scientists realized that it had come from the surface of Mars.

This was not the first Martian meteorite scientists had found on Earth, but it is the oldest. As a result, it is the only meteorite that can tell us what Mars was like so long ago. Scientists hoped it could answer the questions they had been asking for decades.

Martian meteorite ALH84001 is kept at the Johnson Space Center in Houston, Texas.

A Long, Hard Journey

If the ALH84001 meteorite came from Mars, how did it end up on Earth? It's not as impossible as it seems.

Scientists estimate that every year about 2 tons of Martian material rain down on Earth. Most of this material burns up as it passes through Earth's atmosphere, but every now and then, a meteorite made of Martian rock strikes Earth.

Scientists believe that an asteroid hit Mars with astounding force about 3.6 billion years ago. As a result, pieces of rock from the planet's surface were blasted off the surface and went into orbit around the Sun. Eventually, one of these **meteoroids** was knocked out of its orbit and began to fall through space again. About 13,000 years ago, it landed on Earth as a meteorite.

For many years, some scientists had claimed that Mars was once more like Earth than it is now. They believed that when the solar system was first created, Mars and Earth had similar atmospheres. As time passed, however, this changed. Because Mars is much smaller and colder than Earth, its **atmospheric pressure** is much lower. As a result, most of its atmosphere drifted off into space. When Mars began to lose its atmosphere, any water on the surface would have evaporated and formed water vapor. This vapor would have escaped into space along with the rest of the planet's atmosphere. Without water, any life on Mars would have died.

Meteorite ALH84001 was our best chance to see if Mars might have supported life billions of years ago. When scientists studied the meteorite, they noticed something amazing. Within the meteorite's cracks, scientists discovered tiny

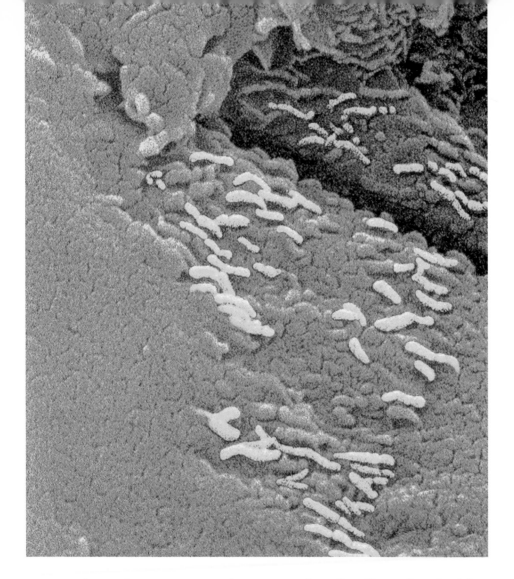

worm-shaped structures that may be **fossils** of primitive microscopic creatures!

Unfortunately, the evidence in the meteorite is not convincing enough to prove that life once existed below the surface of Mars. We will not know for sure whether the meteorite really has signs of Martian life until scientists have more samples to study. Data collected by future missions to Mars may provide the information scientists need.

These color-enhanced, microscopic worm-shaped structures were detected in meteorite ALH84001. Are they a sign that life once existed on Mars?

In 1964, Mariner 4 was launched from the Kennedy Space Center in Cape Canaveral, Florida.

Chapter Four

Space Probes

The first successful mission to Mars was the *Mariner 4*, a probe launched by the United States in 1964. By July 1965, the probe had flown within 6,000 miles (9,660 km) of the red planet. It sent twenty-two photographs of Mars's surface back to Earth. These photos, which gave us our first close-up view of Mars, showed that the planet's surface was covered with craters. There were no Martian cities and no canal systems in any of these images.

Two more U.S. probes were sent to Mars in 1969. *Mariner 6* and *Mariner 7* each flew within 2,000 miles (3,220 km) of the red planet. Photos taken by these probes revealed signs of erosion on the surface.

In 1971 and 1972, *Mariner 9* orbited Mars and took more than 7,000 photographs of the red planet and its moons. These images provided scientists with a very good idea of what the planet's entire surface is like. Many of the images were combined to create a photographic map of Mars. Now it was possible to know—once and for all—whether the planet had any canal systems built by intelligent Martian life forms. After

Mariner 9 *was the first artificial object to orbit a planet other than Earth.*

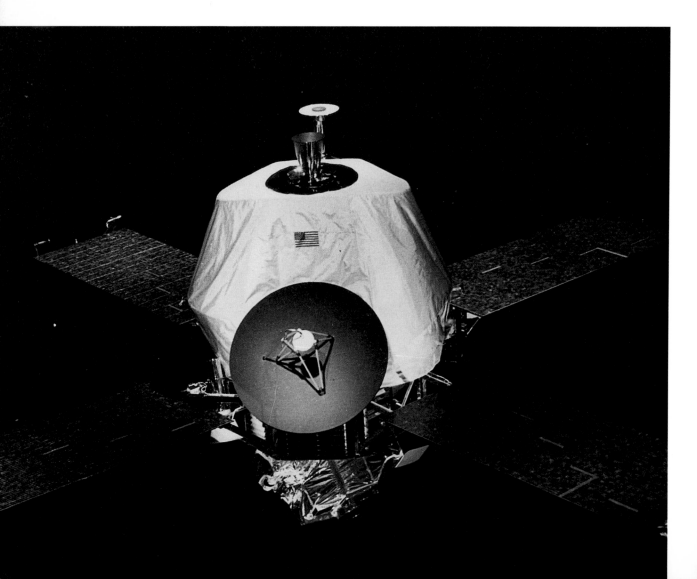

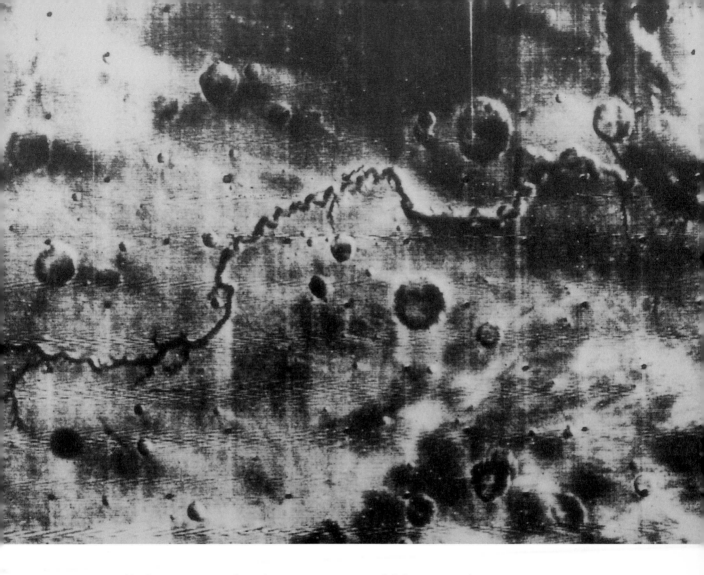

examining all the images closely, scientists could be sure that there are no canals—and no little green men—on Mars.

What had Lowell and the other astronomers seen? Perhaps they'd been looking at other surface features of Mars. Maybe the canal system had seemed real to them because they so badly wanted to believe that other intelligent life existed in the universe. Even though Lowell's theory about Mars was disproved, some of his work helped scientists discover Pluto.

This view of what might be dried up river channels on Mars was taken by Mariner 9.

Viking 1 and *Viking 2*

In 1976, *Viking 1* and *Viking 2*, two unmanned spacecraft launched by the United States, arrived at Mars. Scientists had planned for each spacecraft to land on a smooth area of the planet's surface. When they saw the first photographs taken by the probes, they were quite surprised. *Viking 1* and *Viking 2* had landed in rocky areas. In fact, some nearby boulders were nearly as large as the spacecraft.

This is how we discovered that Mars's windblown plains are covered with huge sand dunes and jagged rocks. Luckily, both spacecraft had settled on relatively smooth terrain. If

This is the first color view of Mars that consists of images taken from the planet's surface.

they had hit a large rock or boulder, the Vikings might have toppled over and been damaged.

The rich variety of rocks found at the landing sites delighted scientists. They came in various sizes and shapes. Some had flat shining surfaces that had been sheared off by heavy ice sheets and worn smooth by blowing dust during Martian windstorms. Many rocks were a rusty orange color. Scientists later learned that a material called **iron oxide**, also known as rust, gave the rocks their color. The iron oxide was present in the soil that coated the rocks. Tiny dust particles of iron oxide in the Martian atmosphere make the planet look red to viewers on Earth.

Both the *Viking 1* and *Viking 2* landers were like small science laboratories. Each one had special equipment to help scientists study Mars. Mechanical arms scooped up Martian rock and soil, and instruments ran tests on the samples. The landers continued to send data to scientists at the National Aeronautics and Space Administration (NASA) until 1982.

Two Spacecraft in One

Each Viking spacecraft had two parts—an orbiter and a lander. The orbiters stayed in orbit around the planet, while the landers landed on the surface.

This color-enhanced view of
Mars consists of many images
taken by Viking 1 Orbiter.

Meanwhile, the Viking orbiters measured the moisture in the Martian atmosphere. They also took temperature readings of the planet's surface. Most importantly, the orbiters took more than 52,000 photographs of Mars's surface.

Between the early 1970s and 1996, only three spacecraft were sent to Mars, and only one—*Phobos 2* launched by Russia—returned valuable data. In 1989, *Phobos 2* took photos of Mars and its larger moon Phobos. Then, a few months into its mission, *Phobos 2* lost contact with Earth.

Even though no important information came from spacecraft during most of the 1980s and 1990s, we were still learning plenty about the red planet. The Hubble Space Telescope, which began to operate in 1993, can't look at Mars as closely as space probes, but it can monitor weather conditions on the red planet. Images taken through this giant telescope have shown scientists that Mars's atmosphere is now cooler and less dusty than it was in the early 1970s.

Images captured by the Hubble Space Telescope renewed the public's interest in space travel and space discovery. As a result, the late 1990s saw a rebirth of the space program.

The Hubble Space Telescope

Our planet is surrounded by a thick atmosphere. The gases in the atmosphere distort what we see when we look into space. They make stars seem to twinkle and planets look fuzzy.

For hundreds of years, stargazers built observatories on high mountains where the air is thinner and the view is clearer. But they always dreamed of having a telescope above Earth's atmosphere. Today, the Hubble Space Telescope, which is about the size of a school bus, orbits Earth and provides us with incredible views of objects inside and outside our solar system.

A look at the Mission Control Center in Houston, Texas

Chapter Five

A New Dawn

On December 4, 1996, a robotic spacecraft called *Mars Pathfinder* was launched into space. After a 310-million-mile (500-million-km) journey, it reached Mars on July 4, 1997. *Pathfinder* had to slow down before landing on Mars. About 37 minutes before it set down on the red planet, the spacecraft began a series of maneuvers that reduced its speed from about 16,000 miles (25,700 km) per hour to approximately 23 miles (37 km) per hour.

Scientists were surprised when the Viking spacecraft landed in rocky areas, but this time they were prepared. The

In this color-enhanced view of Mars's surface, you can see the air bags that protected Pathfinder *as it landed on Mars.*

Pathfinder lander was surrounded by airbags that protected it during a rough landing in an area called Ares Vallis. The spacecraft bounced across the Martian surface for 92 seconds before coming to a stop.

Pathfinder landed less than 30 miles (48 km) from its target. As soon as the lander set down, its solar panels opened and began to collect sunlight. About 90 minutes later, radio signals confirmed that *Pathfinder* had landed safely and was in an upright position.

The *Pathfinder* team at NASA was both relieved and overjoyed. NASA flight systems manager Brian Muirhead said, ". . . it's a proud moment, I couldn't hope for a better beginning." President Bill Clinton called the landing "another exciting milestone in our nation's long heritage of progress, discovery, and exploration."

With its solar panels fully extended like the petals of a flower, *Pathfinder* looked like an oversized blossom. It wasn't long before a camera system rose out of the spacecraft and began taking full-color pictures of the landing site. Because the camera was sensitive to infrared light, scientists on Earth could learn about the chemical composition of nearby rocks and soil by studying the images. *Pathfinder* also carried instruments to measure wind speed, temperature, and atmospheric pressure on the red planet.

A Banner Year

In November 1996, the United States also launched the *Mars Global Surveyor* (MGS). This spacecraft will orbit Mars for more than 2 years and collect all kinds of information. One of its major goals is to photograph and map Mars's surface. It will also serve as a data relay station for radio signals from future Mars landers and atmospheric probes.

This color-enhanced view of Mars's surface is part of a larger panorama taken by the imager onboard Pathfinder *in 1997.*

The Lay of the Land

Scientists believe that Ares Vallis, the area where *Pathfinder* landed, was formed by a great flood that occurred 1.5 million to 3 million years ago. At the height of the flood, the area may have been covered by as much water as there is in all five of the Great Lakes in Canada and the United States. NASA scientists chose this landing site because if the area was once covered with water, it may have supported life.

Ares Vallis may have been a floodplain millions of years ago, but the images sent to Earth by *Pathfinder* showed a dusty basin that looked like Earth's deserts. The bare, stark landscape stretched to the horizon beneath an orange-pink sky. The ground was littered with small rocks and giant boulders.

Nevertheless, it was clear that water had once been abundant there. Pictures sent back from *Pathfinder*'s camera showed clusters of rocks tilted in one direction. These stones looked like those found in rivers on Earth. The photos also showed many smooth, rounded boulders that could have been eroded by fast-moving streams. Similar rocks have been washed down from glacial lakes in the northwestern United States and Iceland.

Erosion on rocks in the area suggest that water may have once swept through the area at a speed of up to 170 miles (273 km) per hour. If this is true, the rushing water probably picked up and deposited rocks as it flowed. As far as scientists were concerned, this made Ares Vallis the perfect landing site.

It meant that the little robot rover on *Pathfinder* would be able to study rocks from many different parts of Mars without traveling too far.

The Robot Rover

The most important piece of equipment on *Pathfinder* was *Sojourner*, a 23-pound (10-kg), six-wheeled robot that looked very much like a toy car. The robot was just 12 inches (30 centimeters) tall and 24 inches (61 cm) long. Many scientists believe that *Sojourner* was the real star of the mission.

Shortly after *Pathfinder* arrived on Mars, *Sojourner* drove down a ramp and onto the Martian surface

This model of Sojourner looks like a robotic toy car.

to begin its work. *Sojourner* operated for more than 30 Martian days, but never traveled more than 30 feet (9 meters) from the lander.

The rover was controlled by a scientist on Earth. The robot transmitted radio signals to the lander, and the lander then relayed them to NASA scientists. Because it took 11 minutes for the scientist's instructions to reach the little rover, *Sojourner* moved very slowly. NASA scientists didn't want it to run into any trouble during the lags between receiving directions.

Like *Pathfinder*, *Sojourner* was equipped with a three-dimensional camera, so that scientists on Earth could view its surroundings. It also had instruments that could test soil and rock. The first object it examined was a dark gray rock just a few feet from the lander. Since the rock was covered with barnacle-like lumps, the *Pathfinder* team named it "Barnacle Bill." Nearby was a large black boulder that scientists called "Yogi."

Sojourner also examined objects a bit farther from the lander. These included a white stone that scientists named "Casper" and a flat rock they called "Flattop." A long, mysterious-looking object was named "The Couch."

Sojourner

A competition was held in schools nationwide to come up with a name for the rover. The winner suggested *Sojourner*, which means "traveler." The student pointed out the connection to Sojourner Truth, an escaped slave who risked her life by returning to the South to help others find their way to freedom. Like Sojourner Truth, *Pathfinder's* rover had to find its way through uncharted territory.

In its travels, *Sojourner* stopped at two hills, which scientists called "Twin Peaks." One of the hills had a white stripe that looked like a ski trail running down a snow-covered mountain. The other hill had four or five bands of rock that reminded scientists of the colored layers of rock in the Grand Canyon. After studying the hills, NASA scientists concluded that they were probably shaped by flowing water.

This color-enhanced view of the red planet's surface includes the rock NASA scientists named "Flattop" (upper left).

The Next Step

Even though the information gathered by *Pathfinder* and *Sojourner* will keep scientists busy for quite a while, NASA is already planning more missions to Mars. Many researchers are

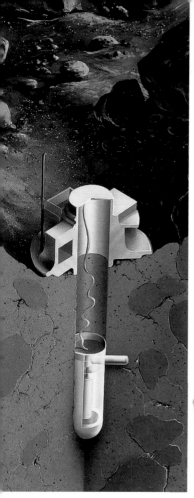

This illustration shows what a microprobe driven into Martian soil might look like. The top portion of the probe will relay information to scientists on Earth.

convinced that what we learn about Mars may tell us more about what Earth was like billions of years ago.

In the future, NASA scientists plan to send a spacecraft to Mars every 2 years. By 2005, they hope to have designed a group of spacecraft that can transport Martian rock and soil samples to scientists on Earth.

If things go according to plan, the first rover sent to collect rock and soil samples on Mars will be nearly five times larger than *Sojourner*. Using a pencil-thin drill, the robot will bore into rocks, find out what they are made of, and place them in a container that can hold up to 100 samples. Two years later, a

Getting Rid of the Germs

Samples from Mars will have to be collected and handled carefully so that they will not be **contaminated** with materials from Earth. To protect the samples, the rovers that collect them—and the containers they are kept in—will have to be **sterile**. If any microscopic creatures accidentally got into the samples, we would never know whether life forms found in the samples came from Mars.

Some scientists do not think the fossil-like structures in meteorite ALH84001 are good evidence that life once existed on Mars because the sample could have been contaminated. These researchers say that it is impossible to know exactly what came from Mars and what came from the ice in Antarctica.

One possible sterilization technique involves spraying the new rovers with hydrogen peroxide gas and then wrapping them in a protective covering that would not be removed until they reach Mars. The gas would kill any living microbes from Earth, and the covering would prevent them from being exposed to any new germs.

Safety First!

Just as scientists will make every effort to make sure that materials from Earth do not come into contact with the Martian samples, they must also make sure that samples from the red planet are not hazardous to us. Researchers don't really expect to find anything dangerous on Mars, but they will be cautious until they have tested the rocks thoroughly.

The Mars lander that has contact with the surface of Mars will never return to Earth, so there is no chance that people will be directly exposed to material from Mars. In addition, the scientists who study the samples will never actually touch them. The samples will be kept in a sealed box and examined through holes with gloves built into them.

second rover will perform a similar mission on another part of Mars.

Several years after that, a third lander and rover will arrive on Mars. The rover will retrieve whichever container of samples seems more promising and place it on the lander. The lander will take off from the surface of Mars and meet up with another spacecraft that is orbiting the planet. The lander will transfer the container to the orbiter, and the orbiter will return to Earth.

An artist's view of a future Mars crew saluting all the people and nations of the world that made their journey possible

Chapter Six

The Future

Sending spacecraft to Mars and collecting samples will teach us a lot about the planet, but these missions are not nearly as exciting as ones that involve sending astronauts to the red planet. Before sending people to Mars, it would probably be necessary to build a base on the Moon. This lunar base would serve as a testing ground for the equipment needed to send astronauts to Mars. But before we can build a lunar base, we must develop a way to assemble it in space.

Because Earth's gravity is so strong, it takes a great deal of power to launch objects into space. The heavier a space-

An artist's idea of what the international space station will look like when it's completed

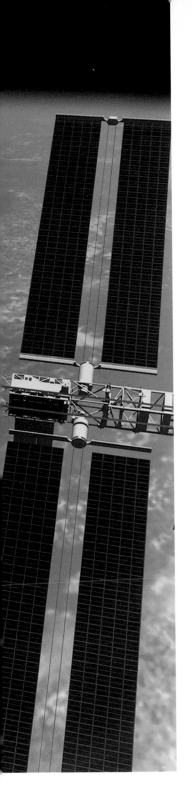

craft is, the more power it needs to escape from Earth's gravity. It would be impossible to launch a complete lunar base into space.

Instead, individual parts must be launched into space separately, put together, and then propelled to the Moon —or, eventually, to Mars. To do this, scientists would like to build a space station. People living on the space station could assemble equipment as well as carry out long-term scientific experiments.

Does a space station sound like science fiction? A group of scientists from the United States, Russia, Japan, and several countries in Western Europe are already building one. If all goes according to plan, the space station will be ready in 2004. Another group of scientists are working to build an unmanned rocket capable of carrying very large pieces of equipment into space. A third group of researchers are developing a National Aerospace Plane—a plane that could take off from a runway, transport astronauts to a space station, and then return to Earth.

Budget Spacecraft

To lower the cost of building spacecraft, airplane parts are sometimes adapted for space travel.

The Cost of Success

Developing such complex space vehicles is an expensive proposition, but many people think they are worth the cost. The researchers involved in these projects do all they can to keep costs down. "Better, faster, cheaper"—that's what NASA administrator Daniel Goldin tells his staff.

Pathfinder was built according to Goldin's goals, and cost $270 million. The 1976 Viking mission cost fifteen times more. Goldin hopes that it will cost no more than $20 billion to send astronauts to Mars. To achieve this goal, NASA engineers will have to find new ways to cut costs while maintaining the astronauts' safety.

To lower the cost of sending humans to Mars, researchers are looking for ways to refuel spacecraft in space. Fuel weighs a lot. A spacecraft that carried fuel for the entire trip would be larger—and more expensive to build—than one that could refuel during its journey.

One possibility is to manufacture fuel on Mars. By developing a lander that can produce rocket fuel from the carbon dioxide in Mars's atmosphere, scientists could begin to create fuel for the home journey before astronauts even arrived. It might also be possible for the same lander to produce enough oxygen for the astronauts to breathe as they travel back to Earth.

Scientists have already started to work on a system that could produce fuel and oxygen on Mars. They plan to test the fuel in spacecraft that carry rock and soil samples—but not people—from Mars to Earth.

Once people can safely travel to Mars, NASA will begin building a permanent base on the red planet. To cut the cost of supporting people on Mars, Goldin hopes the astronauts will be able to grow their own food at the Martian base. Researchers have also suggested that the astronauts may be able to use microwaves to extract water from Mars's frozen areas. They may even be able to mix the water with the planet's red clay-like soil to make bricks and other building materials.

While all these plans may seem like something out of a science fiction novel, they will probably become reality. NASA planners hope that the first humans will be able to visit Mars before 2020. Just think of it—right now you're reading a book about Mars while on Earth. But someday you may be able to borrow a book from a library located on the red planet.

NASA Administrator Daniel S. Goldin at NASA Headquarters in Washington, D.C.

Glossary

asteroid—a large piece of rock that formed at the same time as the Sun and planets.

astrologer—a person who studies the stars and planets and attempts to fortell future events.

atmosphere—the various gases that surround a planet or other body in space.

atmospheric pressure—the force exerted in lower layers of air as the weight of the air at the top of the atmosphere presses down.

axis—the imaginary line running from pole to pole through a planet's center. The planet spins, or rotates, along its axis.

canali—the Italian word for "channel." In some cases, it was mistranslated as "canal," which made people think that the channels were built by intelligent Martians.

comet—a small ball of rock and ice that orbits the Sun. When it gets close to the Sun, some of the ice melts and releases gases. These gases form a tail behind the comet.

contaminate—to infect or make impure by exposure to foreign materials.

crater—an irregular circular or oval hole created by a collision with another object.

dense—containing a relatively large amount of material in a relatively small space.

equator—an imaginary circle around the center of Earth, another planet, or the Sun.

erosion—the process of being worn away by the action of wind, water, or other factors.

fossil—the preserved remains or evidence of ancient life.

gravitational field—the area over which an object's gravity acts. The Moon rotates around Earth because it is within Earth's gravitational field.

gravity—the force that pulls objects toward the center of a planet or other body in space.

iron oxide—the chemical name for rust.

maria—dark areas on the planet Mars; although the word means "seas" in Latin, these regions contain no liquid water.

mass—the amount of matter or material in an object.

meteorite—a meteoroid that hits the surface of another object, such as a moon or planet.

meteoroid—a particle of dust or rock that enters Earth's atmosphere.

orbit—the curved path followed by one body going around another body in space.

rotate—to turn or spin around a central point.

solar system—the Sun and all the objects—planets, moons, asteroids, and comets—that orbit it.

space probe—an unmanned spacecraft carrying scientific instruments that orbits the Sun on its way to one or more planets. It may fly past a planet it has been aimed at, orbit the planet, or, in some cases, even land there.

sterile—pure, or free of foreign materials.

terrain—the physical features of a piece of land.

volume—the total amount of space an object occupies.

To Find Out More

Books

Apfel, Necia. *Voyager to the Planets*. New York: Clarion Books, 1991.

Branley, Franklyn Mansfield. *The Sun and the Solar System*. New York: Twenty-First Century Books, 1996.

Couper, Heather. *The Space Atlas*. San Diego: Harcourt Brace Jovanovich, 1992.

George, Michael. *Mars*. Mankato, MN: Creative Education, 1992.

Getz, David. *Life on Mars*. New York: Henry Holt & Co., 1997.

Graham, Ian. *Space Science*. Austin, TX: Raintree Steck-Vaughn, 1993.

Markle, Sandra. *Pioneering Space*. New York: Atheneum, 1992.

Nicolson, Ian. *Explore the World of Space and the Universe*. Racine, WI: Western Publishing Co., 1992.

Scott, Elaine. *Adventure in Space*: *The Flight to Fix the Hubble*. New York: Hyperion Books for Children, 1995.

Vogt, Gregory. *Mars*. Brookfield, CT: Millbrook Press, 1994.

Walker, Jane. *The Solar System*. Brookfield, CT: Millbrook Press, 1995.

Online Sites

NASA's Quest Project
http://quest.arc.nasa.gov
A list and description of NASA-sponsored educational programs.

NASA Spacelink
http://spacelink.msfc.nasa.gov.
Find all the latest news from NASA at this site.

Welcome to the Mars Missions
http://mpfwww.jpl.nasa.gov
Learn more about *Mars Pathfinder*, *Mars Global Surveyor*, *Mars Surveyor 98*, and *Mars Surveyor 2001*.

Places to Visit

These museums and science centers are great places to learn more about Mars and the solar system.

Flandrau Science Center and Planetarium
University of Arizona
Tucson, AZ 85721

Hansen Planetarium
15 South State Street
Salt Lake City, UT 84111

Miami Museum of Science and Space Transit Planetarium
3280 South Miami Avenue
Miami, FL 33129

The Newark Museum and Dreyfus Planetarium
49 Washington Street
P.O. Box 540
Newark, NJ 07101-0540

Reuben H. Fleet Space Theater and Science Center
1875 El Prado Way
P.O. Box 33303
San Diego, CA 92163-3303

Schiele Museum of Natural History and Planetarium, Inc.
1500 East Garrison Blvd.
Gastonia, NC 28054

Space Center
Top of New Mexico Highway 2001
P.O. Box 533
Alamogordo, NM 88311-0533

Space Center Houston
1601 NASA Road One
Houston, TX 77058

A Note on Sources

It is important to use as many sources as possible when writing a book about space. I began by reading other books written for young people on my topic. Next, I read standard reference works for general information.

Because scientists learn new information about the planets all the time, I read recent articles in a variety of science magazines and relied heavily on information from NASA's Scientific and Technical Information Branch. The Jet Propulsion Laboratory in Pasadena, California, supplied much of the information on missions to Mars.

Many of the facts related to planetary science and the history of Mars exploration came from the Lunar and Planetary Institute in Houston, Texas. In addition, an especially valuable source of information and advice was Jeffrey D. Beish of the Association of Lunar and Planetary Observers who checked the accuracy of this manuscript.

—*Elaine Landau*

Index

Numbers in *italics* indicate illustrations.

About the Author

Popular author Elaine Landau has a B.A. degree from New York University and a Master's degree in library and information science from Pratt Institute.

She has written more than 100 non-fiction books for young people. Although Ms. Landau often writes about science, she has particularly enjoyed writing about the planets. She was fascinated to learn about the major strides the space program has made during the last few years.

Elaine Landau lives in Miami, Florida, with her husband and son, Michael. The trio can often be spotted at the Miami Museum of Science and Space Transit Planetarium.